I0434680

THE INFLUENCER'S CHECKLIST

Tips for Manifesting a More Prominent Leadership Presence

Joel C. Garcia & Miguel (Mike) Garcia

The Influencer's Checklist
Copyright © 2022

International Standard Book Number
ISBN: 979-8-88680-746-2

Printed in the United States, 2022, USA
Booklet $13.95

Dedicated:

To my mom, Teresa Carreon Casas,
5.15.1936 - 3.25.2022,
an immigrant from Totatiche, Jalisco, Mexico.

Your sacrificial life inspired me,
Your influence will always be with me,
And your loving voice will always guide me.

TABLE OF CONTENTS

THE ICON TABLE

Presence

Empathy

Kindness

Conversation

Differences

Joy

Substance

Encouragement

INTRODUCTION

So many of us struggle with building a network of new business relationships or even enriching the ones we already have. As business leaders, we somehow convince ourselves a smaller circle of relationships is far better than enlarging our current universe. Our excuses for engaging in the realm of business networking are limitless. Can you name any reason why you don't get out more to network with others? I list a few reasons I have personally used in the past not to network:

» I am too busy.

» I don't have time.

» I have deadlines to meet.

» I don't get anything from these meetings.

Business growth and profitability are determined by the extent of your relational network. Who knows you even exist? What are the solutions you are offering to others for their business? People won't know unless you show up consistently with a great pitch. If your business is not growing, then you are not getting out there, and making yourself, and your business known to others. This book is about helping you connect better with your prospects, business leads and with your current clients.

This short booklet is about *influence*, and how we can garner a greater measure of it in a short period of time. We reveal eight strategies for helping you build a more prominent leadership presence. We all would like to improve! A warning ahead of time, however, our approach to solving your networking dilemma is from a faith-based perspective. In this booklet we reference various scriptures and reveal biblical anecdotes to help you groom aspects of your leadership presence.

So let's talk about influence, and why it matters in your life, and in your business.

WHAT IS INFLUENCE?

> *Leadership is influence.*
> John C. Maxwell

Influence, we all want it, but just how do we access it? Is influence automatic, does it just happen or do we groom it into existence? Is influence a natural phenomena or a supernatural impartation? Let's first start by defining *influence*. My initial research revealed *influence* is "the capacity to have an effect upon the character, development, or behavior of someone or something."[1] Influence is also the "ability to alter or sway an individual's or a group's thoughts, beliefs, or actions."[2] Influence has the power to impact your thoughts, feelings and actions. For example, someone says something in your hearing, and you take it in. The next day you remember what was said, then all the sudden, you start implementing their advice. A simple smile made in your direction can influence the way you return a similar smile. The way someone dresses up one day can influence the way you will show up the next day. Can you think of other examples? I once heard someone say that we tend to influence at least three people per day without knowing it. Influence happens all the time, and most of the time we don't even know we are influencing others.

---

[1]Merriam-Webster: Influence
[2]Influence; http://www.influencerising.com/What_is_Influence.htm, accessed on 1-21-2013.

We can go on and on with many more definitions about influence, but what do you have to say about the subject of influence. Can you define it in your own words? Go ahead, take a few moments, and write out a short sentence of what you think influence is and does. From my own perspective, I define influence as "a personal catalog of transformative virtues emanating from within, expressed for the purpose of persuading others to embrace a vision, which will harness collective power to create change." Some people are gifted with a natural charisma as a way to influence others. These individuals convey a likable appeal through their personality, and the way they talk to you. Natural charisma or influence is based on one's gifts and talents—it helps momentarily to get you notice, but it will not penetrate fully to make a lasting impact. However, there is something much greater than expressing natural charisma—the influence we will address in this booklet is supernatural in nature.

HOW SPIRITUAL INFLUENCE WORKS: BIBLICAL METAPHORS JESUS APPLIED TO HIS OWN TEAM

In Jesus' day, he embraced common symbols known at the time to explain to his disciples the influence they will soon manifest. Matthew, one of Jesus' disciples, lists the various symbols of influence explained by Jesus:

1. Salt (Matthew 5:13):

"You are the salt of the earth."

What is the purpose of salt? When applied it enhances taste, changes the palette, and acts as a preservation agent. Salt creates more thirst, and people will want more of what you offer. Anything else?

2. Light (Matthew 5:14):

"You are the light of the world."

What is the purpose of light? It exposes what's lurking in the darkness.

3. Yeast (Matthew 13:33):

Even a little yeast can permeate the whole batch of dough and make it rise. In other words, you can rise to influence in your organization by being the yeast, the essential ingredient it needs to expand, create profits and much more. Do your own study about yeast and its function, and consider these questions.

How much yeast does a lump of dough need? A little amount is sufficient.

How is yeast activated to expand the dough? In essence, you are activated the same way, depending upon the situation that is placed before you.

4. Key(s) (Matthew 16:19):

Through revelation Peter received the keys of the kingdom. A key can open and shut a door—a key provides you access into places or can close access. A key gives you authority to enter a new place or apply restraint to those people and things you see unfit.

What do keys symbolize for you?

5. Mustard Seed (Matthew 17:20)

A Mustard Seed is smallest of all seeds (from a visual perspective), yet within time, it grows into a large tree, where the birds of the air are drawn to nest in its branches. Sometimes, your influence will take time to grow before it begins to impact others.

Are you willing to wait for your influence to have an impact?

In sum, influence is:

The life source you carry within you, that manifests an atmosphere through you, which then attracts an audience around you.

6. The Symbolism of Living Waters

Further into my research about influence, I conducted an etymological search for the root meaning of the word influence. To my surprise, my search revealed the root word for *influence* is "a flow of water" and "a flowing into."[3] After reading its original meaning, my thoughts were immediately drawn to John 4:14, where Jesus provided a vivid word picture of spiritual influence with the Samaritan woman at the well, saying:

> *"Whoever drinks the water I give him (**a flowing into**) will never thirst. Indeed, the water I give him will become in him a spring of water welling up (**a flow of water**) to eternal life."*

Jesus promised this woman that a drink of water from Him, a flow of life giving-spiritual waters into her life, would cause her to release an eternal spring from within, and an endless flow of life giving waters to those she would come in contact with. Jesus was referring to spiritual influence before the concept ever entered into our vocabulary. Spiritual influence, which only Jesus can provide you, can enhance your appeal among people, and provide you with supernatural powers, which can be attractive and irresistible. This same offer, the woman at the well received, is meant for you too—to invite you to participate in the greatest adventure of your life. In essence, what you pour into your life, will eventually flow out of your life.

For now, here are a few questions for you to consider:

[3] Influence; http://www.etymonline.com/index.php?allowed_in_frame=0&search=influence&searchmode=none; accessed on 1/10/2013.

» What are you manifesting in your life?

» Have you ever considered what flows out of the well of your life (heart)?

» What do you consume or deposit in your life through your eye gate (sight) and ear gate (sound) that shapes the way you think, behave and interact with others?

» What are you constantly feeding your mind, soul and spirit with?

The answer to these questions should help you evaluate how you are developing your influence.

OUR LIFE'S PURPOSE

The purpose of your life is to live out the abundant life promised and delivered to you by Jesus. Jesus is the life source of this endless stream of living waters known as spiritual influence. These waters are the deep "well" of divine influence bubbling up from within you at the time of your conversion, which continue to manifest a divine stream throughout your life - only if you are able to stay the course by nurturing and guarding its precious flow. Influence is a phenomena which occurs from the inside out. The anointing flowing out from your life is supernatural influence. This divine influence is a person, not a thing, who abides within you, expressing and releasing a supernatural flow of divine favor through you. As my friend Evangelist Sean Smith once proclaimed in one of his penetrative homilies:

> "The flow of water starts with a trickle, but then it turns into a river."

Divine influence starts as a gradual flow of water being poured into your life. It starts with a trickle but, with the proper nurturing it can turn into a mighty stream of refreshing and living waters for everyone who draws from its precious well.

From a practical sense, influence is how we make people feel when they are in our presence. Our presence should have an impact upon them with residual effects. Influence is not complete unless it moves people in all three states of human functionality; intellectually, emotionally and volitionally. Influence is not a tool of manipulation, nor is it something that is forced upon you. Rather, influence is sourced through a life of transparency, integrity and authenticity. Supernatural influence is spontaneous in nature; it is free flowing and it can happen at any given time, when we interact with others. Supernatural influence trumps natural influence each and every time. Anointing, the presence of God in your life, always supersedes natural talents.

CULTIVATING VERTICAL AND HORIZONTAL INFLUENCE – FAVOR WITH GOD AND FAVOR WITH MEN

While acquiring my Master's degree, I wrote an article for Regent *University's Leadership Advance Online*. In this article, I relate how Jesus grew in four key areas; wisdom, stature, and favor with God and man. I dubbed the article *The Four Intelligences of a Leader*[4], where I basically addressed these four qualities of a Jesus' intelligence and influence.[5]

In the article, I include a memorable conversation I had with a friend of mine after the morning 9am service in our church foyer. I was illustrating to my friend how divine favor works in and through a believer's life. In the middle of my vivid illustration, my friend cut me off at mid-stream to tell me about his own bout with divine favor in the marketplace arena. It was obvious to me he had captured the gist of my story. The following testimonial is an excerpt from that article:

A friend of mine was telling me about the 'favor' (influence) he had received from corporate executives of a large grocery store chain on the West coast. Previously, he was unemployed looking for any type of work, so he took a part-time job at a grocery store selling brand food portions to customers from a food cart. Within a few weeks,

---

[4]The Four Intelligences of a Leader, Joel Garcia. Leadership Advance Online – Issue XXII, © 2012 School of Global Leadership & Entrepreneurship, Regent University, ISSN 1554-3757, www.regent.edu/lao. http://www.regent.edu/acad/global/publications/lao/issue_22/4Garcia_intelligence_lao_22.pdf

[5]Luke 2:52

the store manager noticed his product sales go through the roof. This also caught the attention of top brass in the company who eventually offered him a full-time job with a good salary and bonuses. Additionally, he was asked to train local sales managers. He was so good at the initial training sessions that regional and corporate leaders flew in to listen to his sessions. During one of these meetings my friend was asked about the "secret sales magic" he possessed. He simply responded, 'It's a gift from God.' A quick reply came from one of the executives, 'Our company policy dictates you can't bring up your religious beliefs in these sessions.' However, since he had so much favor from the top brass and store manager, they simply allowed him to get by with his antics about God and religion. It seemed they didn't want to disrupt the 'sales magic' he possessed. When you have favor, people will relax their policy guidelines and protocol to accommodate you. My friend finished his conversation with me with a delightful grin on his face stating, 'Next week they are flying me to California to train more corporate leaders. The favor is simply amazing!'

As he talked, I couldn't help it, but to feel the favor oozing out of him. It was simply contagious! My friend had acquired an irresistible like-ability, which garnered him access to people and places he did not have before; and was given unlimited boundaries to speak and to act. This is divine favor (influence) working in and through someone.

My friend was able to access favor from heaven, which also greased the skids for others to extend favor to him, and at times, put up with some of his unusual mannerisms. Favor is the conduit for influencing others. Dr. Lance Wallnau, a prophetic voice in the marketplace arena views favor as a critical component for influencing others. He defines favor as "the affection God has toward you that releases an influence through you, so that other people are more inclined to like, trust and cooperate with you."[6]

So, how can you become a better influencer? This short pamphlet is designed to help you groom a more prominent leadership presence among your audience, your team and those you meet for the first time. So tuck this booklet into your purse or backpack to read it when you travel or when you are at your office. These eight practical tips are proven to be effective devices for influencing others at any given time, including a networking mixer, meeting a new client for lunch or those awkward conversations we often have with strangers sitting next to us on a plane or in a line at a concert.

Let's start with Tip #1 - Showing up whole and healthy with an engaging presence.

[6]Garcia, Joel C. LeaderSphere (2017) Banero books, pg. 60.

TIP #1
AN ENGAGING PRESENCE
Show Up Whole and Healthy

 You cannot influence people you refuse to associate with.

Andy Stanley

The type of influence we are addressing does not happen when you are alone or at a distance. Influence is a phenomena, which takes place when you are fully present with others. Now, there is a time to be present (physically) with others, yet there is something more dynamic than just being present, and that is your presence. Your body can show up for a dinner party but, what people really yearn for is the animated person within you on full display before them. This dynamism is the state of readiness, which we call the *"fullness of your presence"* operating at an optimum level. I will soon explain how influence works in a short story, but first, let's start by defining what presence actually means. A renowned Psychologist defines presence as:

> "Presence is a common experience, but also a mystical one. You can't see it, but you can feel it. It is invisible, but not intangible. Presence is the invisible impact you feel when you are around certain people, places or things."

[1]Merriam-Webster: Influence
[2]Influence; http://www.influencerising.com/What_is_Influence.htm, accessed on 1-21-2013.

He continues:

> "Every person has a presence! Your presence is the most enduring part of your life. It leaves traces of you like an invisible imprint on everyone you meet in life, especially those who are the closest to you. Everyone who encounters you feels your presence when they are around you. And, no one else has a presence exactly like yours."[8]

If no one has a "presence exactly like yours," then you are uniquely wired to influence people in a unique way. Your influence, illuminated through your very presence, is not only in demand in your social circles but, very much needed in the public arena. Therefore, you need to show up "whole and healthy," so you are fully ready to influence others. What I mean by "whole and healthy" is bringing the best version of yourself, the healthy side of you, to the party, not any negativity nor drama. Allow me a short story highlighting this premise about presence to show you how it works in a real life setting.

EXPRESSING THE FULLNESS OF YOUR PRESENCE

There is an obscure story tucked away in ancient literature about man's journey into a town for the first time. Those who were awaiting his arrival had never met him prior to this encounter. The hosts only read about him in a letter preparing them for his visit. Upon arrival, the initial

[8]Ibid, pages 4 & 5.

impressions of this encounter were written down at a later date by the hosts who greeted the mystery guest at the city gate. Their narrative provides us a vivid description of the presence of this new visitor. The host described the visitor as:

> "A man of small stature, with a bald head and crooked legs, in a good state of body, with eyebrows meeting and nose somewhat hooked, full of friendliness (or grace); for now he appeared like a man, and now he had the face of an angel."

Please stop at this point to ponder the visitor's description for a moment:

» By reading this short description, what do you see?

» Was this person attractive by today's standards?

» What made this person so friendly to his hosts?

» What do the onlookers see radiating from the visitor's eyes?

The person giving the new arrival's description was a man known in the Bible as Onesiphorous. Onesiphorous was a Christian referred to in a New Testament letter known as Second Timothy (2 Timothy 1:16-18 and 2 Timothy 4:19).[9] The visitor approaching Onesiphorous at the gate for the first time happened to be the apostle Paul, who was arriving to the city of Iconium from Antioch in Pisidia, areas known today within the region of Turkey. The apostle Paul, prior to his conversion to Christianity was known as Saul of Tarsus, who relentlessly persecuted the early church, but soon, he had a dramatic spiritual experience along the road to Damascus, which converted him from being a persecutor of the church to a convert of Christianity.

The description given by Onesiphorous can be divided into three distinct parts:

A physical description (Body):

Paul was a man of small stature, bald headed, crooked legs (bowlegged), in good physical condition with eyebrows meeting (unibrow), and his nose was crooked (Perhaps broken during a beating).

A tangible and animated soul (Soul):

It is noted, Paul was also "full of friendliness." Another account states he was "full of grace," meaning he extended extraordinary favor and kindness to first-time strangers.

A radiating presence (Spirit):

At first glance, from a distance, he looked like any ordinary man, but when they had a "face to face" encounter, Onesiphorous discerned a distinct glow upon Paul's countenance, much like the "face of an angel."

As you can see from the description given, you don't have to be a male model to be a person of influence. The apostle Paul, according to our modern standards of beauty, falls way below the current standards of a handsome man. However, his physical posture diminished in scope when his friendly nature greeted his hosts at the city gate. I would imagine Paul greeted them with open arms, extending outwardly, much like a gesture of a friendly embrace. Paul's friendly gesture made an indelible impression upon his hosts, who made mention of it.

However, the most lasting impression is evident when Paul drew closer to his host, with a radiating glow permeating through his face and eyes. At the time, the only explanation given by Onesiphorous' of Paul's pulsating appearance (or his presence) was that of "an angel." An old adage notes "the eyes" are the window to the soul. In other words, if true, then Paul was radiating light from within to these first-time greeters.

What had changed in Paul's life, from being known as a belligerent persecutor of the church to now being a stern promoter of its message?

The greatest impression of your influence is not necessarily your physical shape, although at times, it does help to be physically attractive, and dress appropriately for the occasion. Paul's greatest impression was not his friendly nature either, although it caught the attention and affections of his hosts. It was something much deeper within Paul's life, which captivated Onesiphorous' attention—it was the radiating presence of light, which was the very nature of God (God is light, 1 John 1:5) within Paul's life. If you want to be a person who manifests a greater influence, you will need to nurture your spiritual nature more than anything else.

Jesus said, "You are the light of the world." Light, therefore, is an influencing mechanism witnessing of God's benevolent nature living in you. Do you possess this light within you?

Another example of expressing one's inner light to others is found in Hollywood of all places. Do you remember the Tarzan movies of the Golden Age Hollywood film era, mainly the 30's and 40's with Olympic swim star Johnny Weissmuller acting as Tarzan? His co-star happened to be Johnny Sheffield who played his son in many of the movie roles. Upon Weissmuller's death in January of 1984, Johnny, his screen son, spoke at his funeral saying:

> "I can only say that working with Big John was one of the highlights of my life. He was a Star (with a capital S), and he gave off a special light and some that light got into me. Knowing and being with Jonny Weissmuller during my formative years had a lasting influence on my life."[10]

[10]Wikipedia: Johnny Weissmuller, accessed on 12.10.2021

It seems Johnny Weissmuller also exemplified influence, the light shining from within, which had a tremendous and lasting impact upon the life of another human being.

You too, can have this type of influence upon others, by merely getting acquainted with the Master above.

CHECKLIST:
PRINCIPLES OF CULTIVATING AN ENGAGING PRESENCE TO INFLUENCE OTHERS

☑ **Be Authentic:** In the presence of others, just be your unique self. There is no one like you, which makes you a person in great demand. You may not know it, but there is someone uniquely qualified within you others need right now.

☑ **Be Courageous:** Take initiative, greet others, and introduce yourself. Overcome rejection, and let everyone feel your "touch." These things will leave an imprint upon everyone you meet.

☑ **Be Congenial:** Activate your soul to come alive and take action. Speak to your soul and say, "I need you today to show up with love and joy, and to be ready to impart grace to the people you will meet." Be friendly— be likable!

☑ **Be Interesting:** Your life is a mystery; open yourself up more and reveal it; be exciting, hold people's attention, be captivating, and be ready to address different subjects. Each person you meet is a growth encounter;

learn from it, and build your interpersonal skills for the next encounter. Ask questions, listen intently, and glean from others. In other words, have something to say!

☑ **Be Full of Light:** Remember where the core of your influence resides? Allow the light within you to shine forth through your countenance. In others words, let Jesus shine forth through you!

> "The lamp of the body is the eye. If therefore your eye is good, your whole body will be full of light. But, if your eye is bad, your whole body will be full of darkness. If therefore the light that is in you is darkness, how great is that darkness?" - Matthew 6:22-23

TIP #2
EMPATHETIC LISTENING
Making Others Feel Their Value

*One of the best ways to influence
people is to make them feel important.*
Roy T. Bennett

The top skill of any influencer is to listen—you have to start by understanding what a person is trying to convey to you throughout a conversation. You do this by applying a technique called empathetic listening:

> "Empathic listening is a structured listening and questioning technique that allows you to develop and enhance relationships with a stronger understanding of what is being conveyed, both intellectually and emotionally."[11]

Empathy is the emotional part of hearing, where you feel someone through the way they communicate. In other words, can you feel what that person is going through, simply by how they say things with their countenance. The "fullness of their being" should convey what they are saying to you. Listening is the auditory part of hearing and the understanding of the meaning of the words being conveyed.

---

[11]Empathetic Listening: Going Beyond Active Listening. MindTools, Online, https://www.mindtools.com/CommSkll/EmpathicListening.htm accessed on 12.7.202

You can be listening to someone but, not fully understanding them. Empathetic listening is a skill that is acquired and groomed over time through concerted practice. You really have to care about the person in front of you, and be tuned into the conversation before you with empathy. Empathy, which literally translates as "in feeling," is the capability to share another being's personal emotions and feelings.

In a way you have to discipline your hearing to tune into the total discharge of communication; especially the emotional component, as well as, the intellectual side. The nuances, the non-verbals, the reading between the lines, and the actual substance, and the meaning of the words being conveyed all come into play. After all, the ultimate aim of listening is to fully understand what the communicator is trying to convey through complex layers of body, soul and spirit. When you listen with a full understanding, the person before you feels valued. By listening in an empathetic way, we actually show people their worth, that they are sacred and beloved human beings.

Let's start by dissecting the word *understanding* because the ultimate aim of communication is to understand someone fully. Simply put; the object of speaking is to convey a thought, an idea or a point of view. The whole purpose of listening is to gain clarity. To understand someone is to literally to get to the heart of the matter. The word *understanding* can be broken down into two segments:

1. Perceiving what is being communicated

2. Interpreting the substance of the communication

Each of these parts are critical to getting to a place of understanding. To understand, in its basic form, means to "stand under" someone; to literally "walk in their shoes." When we have accomplished this, then we can really say we have empathized with the other person.

Perceiving is the ability to see, to capture, and to seize the moment. For what it's worth, allow me an analogy. My eyes, for instance, are very good at perceiving taste. Wait a moment, let me explain! I may order a steak a certain way, let's say medium-well but, until I taste it, I won't be able to know its true condition. When the dinner plate is put before me, the meal will communicate to me through various levels of visual and olfactory stimulation; mechanisms we also apply during an engaging moment with someone. I then make a judgment and say to myself; I perceive the steak looks good (with my eyes) and smells great (nose). Then it comes down to taste, the climatic end so I know how the steak was really cooked to my specifications. At first, I cut a slice to see what the coloring looks like in the interior of the steak. I want to see if its dry or juicy. Then I place a slice into my mouth, which is already salivating with excitement. There are many steps of perceiving before the steak even enters my mouth. As I begin to chew, I am still perceiving, until the all flavors are released within my mouth.

Now, it is time for the *interpretation*. All the sudden, my palette separates the various flavors of the steak and the gristle with all the ingredients and species added to it to get to the ultimate taste test. I have to interpret the data, then reach a conclusion, which is coming to the place of *understanding*. This is the time when I totally understand how the cook made my steak—the care and attention he or she gave to it while on the grill. I won't actually know it, until I have fully consumed the first piece.

The same process holds true with the perceiving of what is being said in a conversation. Is this person speaking from a place authenticity or disingenuousness, fact or fiction, pride or humility, assertiveness, arrogance or modesty, etc? Communication is like tasting both the gristle and steak at the same time, eventually you want to separate the two, and squeeze out the delicious juices from the steak and spit out the gristle. Perceiving is likewise about discerning what is communicated, so you can separate the various flavors of the conversation, so you can arrive at a distinct place of understanding. Then you can get to that place of empathy; a deep sense of what that person is really going through.

Your attention during a conversation is the valuation you place upon a person. Is the person before you a sacred vessel? Is there something I can learn from them? What is their unique quality that stands out the most? When you actually take the time to listen to someone, where they feel heard and understood, then you have given them a great gift; your time and full attention. You made them feel their worth as a person. For example, I am positive you have been in a conversation where the person is not looking right at you while you are talking to them. For some reason their wandering eyes are looking around into the room while you are still talking to them? It is almost like you don't exist at the moment, right? Then you get the feeling they have got something else on their mind or they are just not tracking with you at the moment. In a conversation, this is what I call "devaluation." You really don't matter to them, do you? It's the worst place to be in. This is why you have to be fully present in a conversation.

Do you remember the previous story (Tip #1), when the apostle Paul arrived to the city of Iconium and greeted Onesiphorous for the first time? Paul was fully engaged; he was fully present with all his mind, soul, body and spirit. I know this by the way he communicated with his whole being. Did you know your whole being communicates all at once? How do I know this? It's the way Onesiphorous described Paul in his short narrative. Onesiphorous starts with a physical description of this body, perhaps reading non-verbal queues from a distance; his walk, physical posture, facial expressions, and so on. Second, he then sensed an animated soul, a person "full of friendliness," was about to greet him. And finally, when Paul got closer, in a "face to face" encounter, the light radiating out from Paul eyes and face captivated Onesiphorous' attention, who perceived the "face of an angel" staring right at him. Everything about you communicates with others all at once, not just your voice and words, but your posture, and your soul (the human side of you) and spirit (the spiritual side of you). This is why you need to pay attention to a person's whole being during a conversation.

CHECKLIST:
SHOWING OTHERS THEY
REALLY MATTER DURING A CONVERSATION

☑ **Posture Up:** Square up with the person in front of you, shake their hand, introduce yourself, focus your full attention upon them, and look straight into their face and eyes. They should be the only person in the room at the time of your conversation.

☑ **Check Your Poise Settings:** Turn on your poise settings, and at times, adjust them. You do this by being graceful and elegant in your demeanor; smile, shake a hand, display warmth and show acceptance; being kind and generous, considerate and empathetic.

☑ **Perceive and Interpret Emotion:** Sense and feel what the person is trying to convey to you. At times, you may need to help clarify their point by asking: "So what you are saying is...?" or "I see, you meant this..., right?" Use your intuition, then clarify, reframe, and affirm them.

☑ **Activate Empathy:** Go beyond the intellect, and feel more. Now, get a sense of what they are going through, of who they are, of what they are trying to convey through their whole being. Get on the same page with them in spirit.

☑ **Promote and Praise Them:** When a person has something substantive to say, promote them by introducing them to someone nearby. "Hey Tom, this is Susie, she's got a great idea about our product promotion. I'll let her tell you about it." Just stand next to them as her promoter and sponsor for a brief moment. Thank them for something in their story, like a testimonial, their sincerity, an insightful truth, wisdom, advice, etc. Find something of value to compliment them on the way out of the conversation.

TIP #3
EXTENDING KINDNESS
Be the Catalyst for Change in Someone's Life

> *Sometimes it takes only one act of kindness and caring to change a person's life.*
>
> Jackie Chan

Kindness is the buzzword of choice being applied on various fronts in the marketplace right now. You cannot avoid it. You can easily find a post about kindness on any of your social media timeline feeds on a daily basis. When I log onto any of my social media accounts, I just need to peruse a few postings and within the top ten posts or so, I will find a post relating to the subject of kindness. It is usually found through someone's story, a picture of someone caring about another person in their time of need or even an inspirational quote about the subject.

Just what is kindness? What does kindness actually look like in a real life setting? According to the Oxford English Dictionary *kindness* is the quality of being friendly, generous and considerate. The word *kindness* is rooted in "courtesy and noble deeds" done to another. The apostle Paul, in 1 Corinthians 13:4, actually references kindness when describing, in detail, the many dimensions of unconditional *love*, starting with...

> "Love is patient, **love is kind**, love does not envy, it does not boast; it is not arrogant or rude..."

When you are kind to others, you are expressing a quality of unconditional love. To take it a step further, extending kindness to another is an action with many residual effects. By being kind you arouse a desire within the recipient to create change for themselves. In essence, they will desire to become more like you. Yes, a kind gesture can upend a person for life. For example, kindness is part of God's nature. The Bible in Titus 3:4-7 and Isaiah 54:10, reminds us of the nature of God; He is kind. When we experience God's kindness, it makes us evaluate our own nature in comparison to His own nature. When we compare our own human nature with His divine benevolence, we then begin to reconsider our own behavior, and desire to make the needed changes in our own life, thus, to be more like Him. Why? The power of extending kindness imparts more than the act itself—it imparts the desire to conform to the other person's nature. When we experience authentic kindness, we feel so loved that we arrive at a place where we desire to change too—to become like the other person in deed and character. When we experience kindness in some way, conviction suddenly sets into our soul, and we begin to think differently about our own selfish ways. So, we go from being less self-centered, to now becoming more centered upon others.

In the book of Romans, the apostle Paul was confronting the gentiles about their ill gotten behavior. He then challenged them to evaluate their own behavior and to consider changing their ways:

"Do you show contempt for the riches of his kindness, forbearance and patience, not realizing that God's *kindness* is intended to lead you to *repentance* (change)?"

Extending kindness to someone is a device for creating change in that person's life. In the passage referenced above, the Greek word for *repentance* is the word metanoia, meaning "a change of mind, thought, or thinking." From a spiritual perspective, this process of experiencing God's kindness impacts a person to reconsider changing their less than noble ways to adopt a better way of living. When we extend kindness to another person, within time, that person will desire to make personal changes too. They will desire to change something about their habits, mannerisms and behavior. The impact of authentic kindness is greater than you think.

Influencing others is about extending kindness to someone, to a level where they feel the impact and eventually desire to be more like you. Extending kindness to some underserving person allows them to re-evaluate themselves. This is the art of influencing others. There is no greater gift than extending kindness to someone. Obviously, in some cases, it will take more than just one encounter of extending kindness to change someone's thinking or behavior. This is why consistency is so vital. Your presence matters in the lives of those around you.

Kindness is a free gift with no strings attached. When you display kindness you are freely giving to a person the fullness of who you are at the moment with no repayment in mind. As the giver, you should not expect anything in return. Influence is about you being the catalyst for change in someone's life. When you influence someone with kindness, you will be in demand in some way. Tony Caiazza, the author of *Shame Breakers*, wrote a profound statement in his book, which immediately caught my attention. He said, "Give to others what they cannot find anywhere else and they will keep returning."

THE LESSON OF A CAPSIZED SEA TORTOISE

Recently, on some social media platforms, I have seen an individual or a group of people attempting to liberate a sea whale or sea tortoise capsized on the beach? If you go to Gisele Bundchen's instagram page (@gisele) you will find a video of her freeing a sea tortoise laying upside down, totally entangled in a green fish net. Gisele's opening line in her post states:

> "Life is a series of opportunities that appear daily, and we chose what to do with them."

Kindness is what we do for those who have no power to do for themselves. The gesture of extending kindness itself, is very rewarding—there is no need for a pat on the back.

Have you been to a networking meeting where a person stands there alone, isolated from certain social circles, which have formed? From a social standpoint it seems as though they've been capsized too. I stand there watching for a few minutes to see if anyone will engage this person in conversation. Sometimes, at a networking mixer, people will often feel like that tortoise on the beach; stranded helplessly alone. Some find themselves frozen or stuck in a place they wish someone would just come over and untangle them out of their fish net. Eventually, I will make my way over to them and engage them in a light conversation. I start off by asking their name. I then follow up with a question, "What drew you to this meeting?" or "What do you plan on getting out of this meeting?" After a few minutes conversing with them, they begin to warm up to you. The next thing you know they are now leading the conversation. In these instances, my goal is simply to take them from a place of separation to participation. I tactfully take them along with me and introduce them to a few people. As I stand next to them, they feel safe and more secure to engage others, since they have already warmed up to me. After a few introductory encounters I just disappear into the mix, and let them unfold before others, much like that tortoise being freed from a net easily returns into the sea. You would be surprised to see how a person just needs a nudge of support before they start to flourish on their own.

BEHIND THE CURTAIN

Showing kindness to someone without looking for a pat on the back or some public recognition is the best form of kindness. Kindness does its best work in the shadows. At times, I will encounter a post on social media where someone did an act of kindness for someone else. I understand their motive—they feel good about their deed. This person will post their story with a picture to inspire others to do the same—they have done nothing wrong per se. However, if you do it for self-recognition, know that self-aggrandizement is not a virtue. Try not to take the credit for a random act of kindness. This takes the focus away from the act of kindness, and puts the spotlight upon you.

You can find this teaching in the book of Matthew,

where Jesus taught his disciples not to clamor for the public spotlight, like the Pharisees were in the habit of doing. Rather, when you do a good deed, like giving your alms to the poor, allow God to reward your kind deed. Jesus advised his disciples:

> "But when you give to the needy [an act of kindness], do not let your left hand know what your right hand is doing, so that your giving may be in secret. And your Father, who sees what is done in secret, will reward you."[12]

How will God reward you? Who knows! But know this, the public accolades will fade within time but, a reward from God lasts forever. An act of kindness done in secret is what God considers great. In time, God will recompense your deed(s) in great measure—it's a promise you can count on.

CHECKLIST:
FIVE WAYS TO EXTEND KINDNESS

☑ **Be friendly:** Embrace people unconditionally without any prejudice or judgment.

☑ **Be considerate:** In the moment, put people's needs above your own. In your interaction, you should want more for that individual. Figuratively speaking you need to bring them to the front of the line per se. Elevate them don't devaluate them in any way.

☑ **Be graceful:** Showing someone grace is showing them you like them, and that you favor them. You want them to move forward and win with great success.

☑ **Be generous:** Be open handed with people; give of your time, talents and treasures to that person in front of you. We all have the power to be generous, and offer an open hand to others.

☑ **Be hospitable:** Show warmth, welcome people, make them feel valued and appreciated. Serve their needs first; "Hey, can I get you some water?"

TIP #4
ELEVATING THE CONVERSATION
Bringing the Conversation to a Higher Place

> *Influence is our inner ability to lift
> people up to our perspective.*
>
> Joseph Wong

Most of us have attended business mixers or meetings of some kind in the early morning hours, at lunch time or in the evening hours after work. If you are a regular attendee at these sort of events, then I am sure you have had those conversations, which have gone south in some way. You got the guy with no filter, who tells a dirty joke in the presence of a lady. There is no evidence of social etiquette nor awareness, right? It seems as though decency has left the building, and you are left in an awkward position. And, to fit in with the group, we often feel the need to "go along to get along." So we laugh at an off-colored joke, at the sacrifice of our own conscience and those among us. Now, I am not against humor but, there is a proper place and time for the office Court Jester.

I think the worst conversations come in the form of gossipy and juicy content. Just by standing in a line to board a plane or at a coffee shop you can overhear others speaking on the phone about a colleague at work, which makes you wonder about humanity at times. Jealousy and envy lead people to talk about others in strange ways. Some of the content maybe true but, most of it is exaggerated, embellished or hyped up to make one look superior.

So how can we change the focus of the conversation into something more agreeable and professional? First, allow me to list a few transitional techniques, which can help you bunny trail off into a different direction when a conversation goes south on you.

TRANSITIONING OUT OF CONDESCENDING CONVERSATIONS

People who appropriate moral awareness to a certain situation are capable of transitioning out of an inappropriate conversation to salvage the grief, which may arise from its ignoble content. There are tools you can use to transition out of a condescending conversation and take it to a higher place. For one, you can...

1. Redirect the flow

An influencer can steer the conversation in a different direction by appropriating something like, "Hey, you think that's funny, listen to this..." This technique should make others aware of the gossip, vulgarity or indecency before them. You should then tell a story about what happened to you recently. This way you are steering the flow of conversation in a different direction much like a car does when it makes a left or right turn on the road.

2. Inject a new flow

You can influence the conversation by injecting your own ideas, opinions and thoughts about an aspect of the subject matter at hand. This way you take the focus off the degenerating content and move the conversation in a different direction. The goal is to get others to join into a new flow.

3. Reject the current flow

This is a harsh way of moving out of a less than desirable conversation by simply saying, "Hey, let's move on to something else, we are getting into some shady areas here." This is quite the courageous move. Influence is not always about being nice, but about being morally right.

What other ways have you personally steered a conversation into a different direction?

TRY SEASONING THE CONVERSATION WITH SOME GRACE

I have found that applying "grace" into your conversations will garner you a greater measure of influence. Grace means extending someone unmerited favor. In other words, a person may not actually deserve your kindness, time, nor attention, for whatever reasons, but you extend it to them anyway. Grace means you are for them, not against them. For example, I remember telling two different people, at different times, about an encounter I had with a Psychic. The Psychic, who stood in line behind me, basically told me, "Hey, I am getting some vibes from you." Testing her, I said, "What kind of vibes?" She volunteered two things that did not hit home with me, but her technique was a way for any gullible person to ask for more. If someone makes a general statement like, "You are having financial problems." You may buy into it, since many of us, currently or at some point in time, have experienced some financial challenges. Then she went on to say she was opening up a new office, and that I should stop by to receive a deeper reading. I knew it was nothing more than a business ploy to increase the traffic at her new office. As a Christian, this encounter did not bother me one bit. The Psychic was not a threat to me nor to my faith.

So on separate occasions, I shared this encounter with two of my friends. They both responded in two different ways. The first person responded in a way where I gladly received their feedback. His response was not condescending at all but, full of empathy and understanding. He basically said, "This is what I would've done..." and went on with his advice. He didn't shame me in anyway. The second person, however, immediately stated, "You should've known better..." and went on to give me a prescriptive response. This person didn't stop there, they went on and on, about how to do it right the next time. It was like I didn't get this person's point after the first go around—they just kept hammering away. As you can see, I felt quite different from the second person's response. I felt shamed, and inadequate, like I fell short in some way of the opportunity presented before me. And perhaps I did in some respects. As you can see, I didn't receive the advice from the second person at all. It had an adverse affect upon me and repelled me, instead of drawing me in.

This is the very reason why your conversations should be seasoned with grace.[13] For a conversation to be laced with grace means the truth should be presented to the listener in a pleasant and pleasing way. Have you ever put salt on your food? Why do you do it? You do it to add or enhance the taste of the bland food entering into your palette. The same principles holds true in a conversation. When you add some seasoning into your conversation or respond in graceful manner, the hearer will be able to receive your input much better. Grace means you extend them favor. In other words, you avoid being harsh and direct with the truth. In this sense, you are not being condemning in any way, but by accepting their shortcomings, you frame your response in a way they will actually receive and be responsive too. Paul tells his audience the following:

"Let your conversation be always full of grace, seasoned with salt, so that you may know how to answer everyone." - Colossians 4:6

A conversation is really a delicate balance between telling the truth with grace.[14] Truth can be a hard pill of medicine to swallow at times, because by its nature it is often offensive. Truth can be direct and harsh at times. This is why grace is applied when conveying truth in a conversation. Grace is the full embrace of an individual regardless of their weaknesses. Therefore, salt is the ingredient you apply to make your conversation more appealing to the listener. When this happens, the truth can penetrate the heart and mind quite differently with greater effect.

Do you remember this song lyric from a famous 1960s movie, it goes something like this:

"A spoon full of sugar makes the medicine go down."

Truth is much like taking a spoonful of medicine. A person knows they need it but, how do you get them to swallow the bitter side of the medicine? You have to coat the medicine with sugar, right? The added ingredient of sugar just happens to be how grace works in a conversation—it softens the blow of truth. Only then, are you able to vanquish the bitterness of the medicine as it enters the palette.

[14] John 1:17

CHECKLIST:
HOW TO SEASON YOUR CONVERSATIONS WITH GRACE

☑ **Be Aware:** Be aware of the relationship before you. All relationships have value. The key is how you respond to the person sharing with you.

☑ **Pause and Reflect:** Don't be impulsive with your initial response. Pause for a moment, and reflect on how you will respond. It takes a few seconds to search for wisdom. Adopting a "be quick to listen and slow to speak" approach can save you the embarrassment.[15]

☑ **Wrap the Truth in Love:** Speak the truth in love.[16] Love is what? Read 1 Corinthians 13 to understand the different facets of love.

☑ **Deliver the Truth Favorably:** Have you ever been "tongue whipped" but didn't know it until later on? My wife is gracious, more often than not, with her advice. I feel kindness coming through at first, but later on, I can feel the truth hitting me square on the nose. Truth is better received when it has a time lapse effect to it before it strikes you.

[15]James 1:9
[16]Ephesians 4:15

☑ **The Goal is Edification:** The goal in a conversation is to edify a person, which means to build them up from within, to enlighten or inform them, not to condemn them in anyway.

TIP #5
EMBRACING THE DIFFERENCES
Not Everyone Will Share Your Worldview

> *Tolerance implies a respect for another person,*
> *not because he is wrong or even*
> *because he is right, but because he is human.*
>
> John Cogley

The two subjects most divisive in any conversation are simply politics and religion. Unless you know those among you, and you are in agreement with them, then these subjects are fine to address in a mixer or a networking meeting. However, there will be times when not everyone in the room or in your circle will share your worldview. There will be differences of opinion among you in many subjects, including politics and religion. So you must learn to embrace the differences without compromising your own values. In this process you will need to possess a level of awareness, discernment and some measure of compassionate restraint before you speak.

Jesus provided you and I a life metaphor to teach us how to read our environment, and therefore, to help us shape our awareness in social circles. Jesus taught his disciples to "be as shrewd as serpents and innocent as doves."[17] What was the meaning of this metaphor in their day? And, how can we appropriate this teaching in our day? This is what is said about serpents:

Snakes receive information about their surroundings by interpreting chemical signals given off by potential prey. Snakes are able to sense their prey by picking up chemical information from the air with their tongues. When a snake flicks its tongue in and out, it can detect its prey's scent trail.[18]

When you enter into a room you should try to activate this detecting feature. Try not to stick out your tongue, when you walk into a meeting, haha! How do you apply this teaching in a professional setting? You apply it by using your intuitive senses to read the room and pick up stimuli from the atmosphere and those around you. Intuition is embedded in our spirit nature. When our spirit is awake and active, we have a greater awareness to pick up on the vibes around us. Ask yourself some of these questions the next time you enter a networking meeting:

» What is the vibe here?

» Is the atmosphere hostile and cold?

» Is the space I am entering spiritually lifeless?

» Is it friendly or uninviting?

<◦ ◦>

 What Senses Do Snakes Use To Catch Their Prey? By Lisa Miller, online at https://animals.mom.com/senses-snakes-use-catch-prey-10570.html, accessed on 12.6.2021.

» Do I sense enthusiasm and energy in the room?

» Is there a sense of excitement or dread in the room?

This is just the beginning, then it comes down to conversations with each individual or those around you at your table. What are you sensing among these smaller groups or the person next to you? Picking up stimuli from your environment, much like a snake in their own environment, helps you get an idea of the spiritual climate in the room.

Now, the next phrase of Jesus' teaching says to "be gentle (innocent) as doves," which simply means to be highly sensitive to the environment around you in a calm and cool demeanor with collective restraint. A snake can sense its atmosphere, whereas, a dove is undaunted by it. The dove remains aware of the climate, but for some reason, it abides in stillness and peace, knowing it can take flight at any given moment.

Are you able to stay calm and collected in an adverse atmosphere?

By possessing both attributes, you will know what you are walking into to get the full picture, so that you can navigate the crowd and influence the people in the room in a greater way.

THE POWER OF EMPATHY AND COMPASSION

Empathy is a powerful tool to understand, so you can respond in an appropriate way. For some people "sensing and feeling" what others are going through comes naturally, for others you have to cultivate it, in order to grasp how it works. Empathy should exist, to some extent, in everyone's social toolbox. The normal shift from feeling empathetic towards someone's story is shifting your power from feeling to action. Empathy moves us to action, because we understand. Understanding a person needs is the primary objective of empathy. Once we understand someone's story, we can move into action on their behalf. This is where compassion comes into play. You see, empathy cares and compassion cures! Before you can "cure" someone, you have to show them you really "care." If you fall short of "caring" for someone you will not be able to give them what they truly need, which is a "cure." A cure is the right remedy to redeem them from their troubles.

Embracing the differences among you and another person does not mean you agree with that person's viewpoint or lifestyle. It simply means you understand their worldview, and apply compassion. I love conversations where two people stand so far apart in their beliefs but, by the end of their conversation, they have moved closer to the center with a greater proportion of understanding and respect for each other's viewpoints. Civil discourse has been rare these days. Some people are too sensitive and easily enraged to even move to the center. Coddling others will never help them mature in character nor into adulthood. The truth sets you free, right? But the truth has to be seasoned with grace and love to have greater impact.

Embracing the differences basically means being able to converse with someone without losing it, and to connect with someone without judgment. Embracing the differences is the ability to respect another's viewpoint, without being disrespectful. Embracing the differences is embracing someone fully with great understanding and compassion for their worldview.

CHECKLIST:
FIVE WAYS TO EMBRACE THE DIFFERENCES

☑ **Be Understanding:** Empathy cares, compassion cures, right? We first have to understand someone, before we can take action or not.

☑ **Find Common Ground:** Common ground is the area of agreement. Avoid the extreme viewpoints that do not build others up. Some conversations need to stay in the middle.

☑ **Be Affirming:** Be affirming when you do agree with someone. This tends to minimize any resistance and reduce the distance between you and the person in front of you.

☑ **Apply Seasoning:** Add grace and salt to the conversation; be pleasant and kind when conveying your thoughts and opinions.

☑ **Love Never Fails:** Unconditional love is the remedy for all things. When a person feels unconditionally loved, they will feel safe in your presence. When love is present, your wisdom will resonate within them in due time. Let love do its work, when you cannot!

TIP #6
EXPRESSING JOY
People Should Draw Strength from Your Presence

 *Our influence is determined
by the quality of our being.*
Dale Turner

Joy is expressed from a deep well of gratitude. Many times this joy is cultivated by overcoming our own trials and tribulations. When we go through a difficult time, something is squeezed out of us in the process, albeit, a renewed character and hope for a better future. When we overcome a trial we receive a renewed hope from heaven that the future will be better, and therefore, joy becomes a constant and expressive companion. So the next time you go through a difficult time, know that you have traveled through this pasture before, but now you know there is light at the other end, and that light is usually the dawn of a new day.

There is a difference, however, between joy and happiness. Happiness is a state of being derived from how well you are doing at the moment. Happiness can be unstable at times, because it depends upon your emotional well being, and the stability of your environment. Whereas joy springs forth from a deep well, which bubbles up within you during the good and hard times. The product of joy is receiving an inner strength. When you express authentic joy, you exude a strength others will desire for themselves, so they can confront their own challenges head-on. Joy provides us the strength we need to move through difficult situations.

Joy cannot be manufactured; it is cultivated through how we deal with the challenges we have faced and have overcome. Joy springs forth from being spiritually refined through trouble. Somehow, we got through something difficult in our life, so we can overcome it again and again. The next time a challenging time comes our way, I know I will be the victor not the victim. When we get to the other side, we are able to look back and see what became of us, and this evaluative summary deposits a new strength within us.

Joy is like the ripe fruit on a tree—it is tangible, agreeable and ready to consume. In other words, those who are among you are able to see it in your life, and access it for themselves. Happiness, however, lasts for a moment—it's a temporary emotion of appeasement. One day you feel one way, then the next day you are back in the same depressed state as when you started. When you carry and express authentic joy in your life, you are expressing the resilient strength of an overcomer. Your inner strength then becomes contagious, touching the lives of those around you, and moving them deeply to face and overcome their own dilemma.

Have you ever seen a person suffer? I mean they have been through loss after loss, and for some reason, they manage to display a sunny disposition through it all. What is their secret formula for survival? What makes them move forward with resiliency? The answer is simple. They make it through the valley of despair knowing hope is around the corner. Hope is the great anticipation that a better future awaits them. We all have gone through some sort of struggle, which is why we can relate to others who have gone through similar circumstances themselves.

When Jesus went through his final trial at the cross, he was given a view of the future. He was given a glimpse of the outcome of His struggle. This perspective strengthened His resolve to move forward with the final mission. This portal into the future caused Him to see the outcome of His actions were greater than His current challenges. For the joy set before Him, He endured the cross and scorned its shame.[19] When we possess authentic Joy, we too, can handle the most difficult of circumstances set before us.

A smile is not necessarily an expression of joy. People can be sad on the inside and still smile on the outside. Candid humor is not always a release of joy. Humor can be a facade, which oftentimes conceals the pain a person holds inside. Joy is not an "off and on" switch—we feel one way a

$$\diamond\!\!-\!\!\diamond\!\!\diamond\!\!\!\!\!\!\!\!\!\!\!\!\!\!\!$$

certain moment, and then, in the next moment we disguise our countenance to look acceptable in the presence of others. These are temporary masks. Joy is not temporary— Joy is eternal. Joy is an expression of an inner strength from a resilient life.

Doctors tell us you will live longer if you are joyful. Here is a list of the many benefits of joy:

» Laughter, an expression of joy, boosts the immune system.

» Joy speeds the heart rate and improves blood circulation.

» Joy increases antibodies combating infections.

» Joy causes the body to secrete an enzyme that protects the stomach from forming ulcers.

» Joy alleviates depression, lowers blood pressure, reduces stress, increases the oxygen level in our blood, and gives us a sense of well-being.

» Joy immeasurably increases our enjoyment of life.[20]

Do you remember the story in the Bible of the women who had a rare blood disease?[21] She had *suffered* with constant bleeding for twelve years—it was literally incurable. Until the day she saw Jesus walking in the crowd, she knew immediately what to do. For reasons of her own, she just had to get close to him, to touch at least the hem of his garment as the crowd pressed upon him from all sides. She knew in her heart by just touching him, she would be healed. This is

 [20]Taken from a sermon by Robert Heidler of Glory of Zion, Corinth, Texas, 2/2022.
[21]Matthew 9:20-22

how faith works. When she pressed through the crowd and finally stretched herself to touch the hem of his garment, she was immediately healed. However, another interesting thing happened. Jesus felt the healing virtue flowing out of him, like someone had made a "withdrawal" from his person. Jesus was on his way to heal someone else. The woman was not His target at the moment, but she made Jesus her target, knowing full well He was the solution to her suffering. He then turned and asked, "Who touched me?" His disciples responded, "Lord, there are many pressing against you. Why do you say who touched me?" But, Jesus knew the healing virtue he carried within himself had gone out of him. At that moment, the woman with the issue of blood felt convicted, so she came forward to confess. As she drew near to him, she confessed everything. She admitted that she was the one who had touched the hem of his garment.

This woman, by faith, made a withdrawal from the healing virtue Jesus carried within himself. So she accessed a life giving source from the Master's deep well, and joy filled her heart for the rest of her life.

You too, carry a life giving source of virtue for others—it's called joy. When you express joy, others will be naturally drawn to you, to tap some measure of it out of you for their own good. They too will draw strength from this divine source of influence you carry within you.

CHECKLIST:
FIVE WAYS TO EXPRESS JOY

☑ **Express the Character of Joy:** The next time you go through a difficult time, know that better days are just ahead. Therefore, trust the process of a trial to cultivate a new character within you. The product of this renewed character is joy. Joy allows you to live the life of an overcomer!

☑ **Joy is a Fruit of the Spirit:** The Bible speaks about "joy" being a fruit of the Holy Spirit. Fruit is the natural product of a healthy tree. When your spiritual root system is healthy (the inner core of your being), your life will bear good fruit. Part of this fruit is joy. Allow the Holy Spirit to cultivate the spiritual fruit known as joy.

☑ **Display Joy in Your Own Testimony:** Allow your life to be a testimony to others. Don't let a personal tragedy define you and your personal worth. Let others know they can be triumphant through all seasons and challenges of their life.

☑ **Joy is Contagious:** Joy is not contrived; it is contagious. Contrived joy only masks the pain, while authentic joy imparts strength to others. You will know when you have experienced authentic joy, your resolve to move forward becomes greater.

☑ **Joy Imparts Strength:** Joy is eternal. It is an attribute of heaven's personality. When you live out true joy, you are expressing an attribute of the divine nature.

TIP #7
EMPLOYING SUBSTANCE
A Time to Show Your Self-Worth

> *The ability to influence people without irritating them is the most profitable skill you can learn.*
>
> Napoleon Hill

An influencer is patient to wait their turn, for the right moment to speak on their own behalf. I have attended many networking mixers. I know how limited in time mixers and networking meeting can actually be. They usually last one to two hours, which is not enough time to get your brand out there. After all, the purpose of going to a networking meeting is to show off your self-worth right? The recognition of who you are, and the affirmation of what you do, is critical to your viability and success in business. We have been taught to be polite, and not to be too pushy with our agenda nor talk about ourselves too much. Eventually, in a networking meeting, you will need to talk about yourself at some point in time, and to pitch your business, project or idea. You don't want to be too hasty and miss the way.

Not only have I been to various types business mixers throughout the years. I have also started and sponsored one for about two years. I called my business mixer group Business and Bagels. It was a morning business mixer, which was well attended each month. I remember putting a stop to it for personal reasons, and those who regularly attended really missed these monthly gatherings. During my experience attending and growing my own business mixer, I learned that pushing your agenda too fast or your brand too hard will only turn off potential prospects. Arrogance and smugness is not something you want to be known for within your business circle. This is why "patience with a plan" is the best strategy for getting yourself noticed. After all, a key attribute of an influencer is possessing patience, right? It takes time to develop a strategy to make the connections you so desire. After you make a good connection you have to nurture the relationship by building credibility and trust overtime. Trust is the gold standard in any business relationship. You don't want to harm your brand right away by being too pushy. There will come a time to show off your self-worth. You will just have to wait for the right timing and the critical "open door" moment to speak.

The Greeks were known as the wordsmiths of language. They became the creators and the experts of "root word" meanings, which laid the foundation for our language today. They revealed a concept known today as *Kairos*, which can be construed as the "right, critical and opportune moment."[22] Kairos, therefore, signifies a proper or opportune time for action; a short, important and critical window in

[22]Wikipedia: Kairos

time to take action. This is why discerning the right moment to show your self-worth matters. Allow me a quick story to explain how the concept of Kairos works with opportunities before you and those you will engage with.

I had an unusual encounter with a U.S. Senator at the Reagan—Washington National Airport in Washington D.C. I was returning from a ministry trip in Vermont, and catching a connecting flight back to Las Vegas, Nevada. All the sudden I heard a voice cutting through my thoughts and interrupting them saying, "You are going to meet a Senator." I knew it was God speaking to me, so I shared my divine moment with a traveling companion who was standing next to me. This is what I call a "God encounter." When God speaks to me in this manner, I know I am being commissioned as His ambassador to convey His heart and purpose to another person. Within a few minutes, we witnessed the U.S. Senator from our home state pass right by us. As he looked over at us, he nodded a nonverbal "Hello!" Since I was in charge of the special guests at my church, we hosted this particular Senator during many of our patriotic holidays, mainly on Memorial Day weekend and the 4th of July, to give a speech on the importance of faith in connection to freedom.

After I made eye contact with the Senator, I turned to my traveling companion and said to him, "He's the one! I need to go over and speak to him." This was my time for action; a short window of time to chat with our Senator before boarding our flight. It was my Kairos moment. So I walked over and greeted him. He exchanged the greeting and remembered me through our previous encounters. This was a connection (Tip #1) ordained by God. So I knew there was a message He wanted me to convey to him. After talking for a few minutes, the Senator asked me a question, "Do you know what the apostle Paul was called to do?" I paused for a moment and immediately answered his question; the apostle Paul was called to government (among two other specific groups, the Jews and the Gentiles). I immediately saw his facial expression light up with my quick reply. The reason for my quick reply was that I taught the book of Acts in our Bible school several times, so I was familiar with Paul's calling. And, this book of the Bible just happens to be my favorite subject to read and teach. The Senator responded, "I have asked other pastors the same question, but they don't know the answer. You answered it right away." At this time, I knew I had his attention. I had built immediate credibility and trust. So I discerned this was my "open door" to ask him a question. So I asked him, "Senator, are you going to run for office again." He responded, "I don't know yet. It's hard being away from my wife and family for long periods of time." I then encouraged him to run again, adding my personal commentary, "The country needs you, Senator! You are one of the solid conservatives we have in Congress." Soon after, we boarded our flight. We each had a different seating arrangement, so I was unable to continue the conversation but, I felt at peace knowing I had delivered the message God wanted me to convey to him.

Did you know he decided to run for office one more cycle? He actually won his seat with over a 50% margin of the vote in Nevada! He was the only conservative Senator who won his race in a year when President George W. Bush lost the House of Representatives and the Senate. The Senate was split 49 to 49 with two independents completing the full 100 seat senate for the next two year term. When I look back at this moment, I cannot believe God used me to influence someone at the national level. In this instance, I took advantage of a Kairos moment, which was offered to me. I stepped into the moment, and filled the vacuum with my knowledge and wisdom. I, therefore, was able to "employ my substance" at the right time, at the right place with the right person.

There will come a time when you too will discern your Kairos moment. Will you be ready to enter into your moment in time, and impart your knowledge and wisdom?

Substance is the cumulation of the knowledge and wisdom you have gained throughout your years of learning and experiencing life. Substance is not only what you carry within you that matters, but how you go about conveying it to others. Communicating resonating wisdom at the right time, with the right people will surely get you noticed. I have learned that leaving someone wanting for more of what I have to say is a way to get them thinking about me. However, leaving someone more empowered for their future is the key to successful influencing. Have you ever had someone search you out by asking someone you know for your phone number? I have had my friends refer me over to someone I had met at their party. They said something like, "Hey, this guy asked for your number, I hope you don't mind." They were seeking after me because of the 'substance' I carried with me—the wisdom and knowledge I had accumulated and conveyed at some point in our encounter. So they searched me out for more of it.

A TWELVE YEAR OLD BOY

There is story in Luke of a twelve year old who interacted with top biblical scholars for a few days. The scholars who met with him were "amazed at his understanding and his answers."[23] In other words, Jesus, as a pubescent, not only had delivered substance at twelve years of age, he delivered a wisdom beyond his years, which amazed his audience. They key was simple—Jesus first listened to what they had to say, then at the right moment, sounded off with resonating wisdom of his own. Right after this encounter, it is said of Him that He "grew in wisdom and stature, and in favor with God and man."[24] In what key areas are you currently growing in your life?

⟨◦⟩

[23]Luke 2:46 & 47
[24]Luke 2:52

Jesus grew in four areas of substance:

» **Wisdom:** A combination of knowledge and the understanding of reality, people and life in general. Wisdom is also an impartation from the Master above— its spiritual in nature. God invites us to ask Him for more of it, so we are able to influence at a greater measure. When you ask, believe in faith you have received it, and it will flow out of you.

» **Stature:** A combination of physical growth, along with the maturity of character for each stage in life; from childhood to youth, and from youth to adulthood, we should display a measure of maturity in keeping with age.

» **Favor with God:** He grew spiritually, and matured in his faith, which brought about God's approval and favor upon his life. God's favor is essential for influencing others.

» **Favor with Men:** He became a likable person around others, so he gained their favor. When God's favor rests upon you, it is naturally evident to others. Favor with God makes you favorable and attractive to others.

If Jesus astounded the Scribes of his day at the age of twelve, what happened much later when he became an adult? First and foremost, Jesus possessed an authority to speak, because "he taught as one who had authority, and

---

not as their teachers of the law."[25] Second, no one could debate nor argue against him. The Pharisees, Sadducees and the Scribes could not stand up to his wisdom nor his rhetoric. Jesus owned every stage he stood upon. One time, after a question and answer period, the narrative in Matthew notes, "No one could say a word in reply, and from that day on no one dared to ask him any more questions." This is what I mean when a person employs substance in a conversation. Those around you will recognize your wisdom and authority. They will know you are a substantive person, and will seek you out.

<u>CHECKLIST:</u>
<u>HOW AND WHEN TO SHOW YOUR SELF-WORTH</u>

☑ **Let Others Speak First:** Listen, as others lead the conversation, eventually your turn will come up. Waiting is the difficult part when you have something of true substance to say.

☑ **Track the Conversation:** Make sure you are tracking with others by listening and digesting the content of the conversation. It would be a mistake if someone turned to you, and asked for your input, and you were caught off guard, not knowing the substance of the conversation.

☑ **Wait for an Open Window:** Your opportunity will arise at some point in the conversation. Eventually, that Kairos moment to speak into the subject matter will arise.

☑ **Let Wisdom Talk:** Wisdom will always bubble up within you at the right time, then you will have something to say. When will you know? It will flow naturally out of you with substance.

☑ **Show Your Worth at the Right Time:** Wisdom spoken at the right time will never let you down. Your worth will be noticed and admired by others.

TIP #8
EXITING WITH ENCOURAGEMENT
Deposit Hope Upon Departure

> *Be around people who have something of value to share with you. Their impact will continue to have a significant influence.*
>
> Jim Rohn

All gatherings and business mixers must come to an end at some point. Your main objective before you leave someone's presence, a group or a meeting, is to deposit an encouraging and edifying word that imparts hope to your audience. Why an encouraging word? An encouraging word leaves people edified, emboldened, and strengthened with a resilient hope to face the future. When you encourage someone, you are filling up their emotional tank, and igniting a spark of motivation into their soul. In other words, through your encouraging words you reinvigorate others to embrace their present dilemma, so they can look forward to a better future with renewed confidence.

What does encouraging someone look like? Before we can answer this question, let's take a look a few hidden devices that cloak themselves in the form of encouragement. These devices are know as charm and flattery. Let's start with charm.

CHARM

A person who charms, in a sense, is using an ancient magical device to influence you. Don't get me wrong, some people are naturally charming, while others use charm to concoct a false image of themselves to present to others. The word *charm* is associated with magic, the chanting or reciting of a magic spell or a practice or expression believed to have magical powers.[26] In Proverbs 31:30, we learn "charm is deceptive," much like "beauty is fleeting." As beauty fades within time, charm's duplicity will also be unveiled within time. But, until the unveiling happens, there is a window where you can fall prey to a charmer. Have you ever said something like, "Oh my, he is so charming." I understand what you are saying; you are trying to compliment someone for their appeal, approach, and attraction. However, charm falls within the arena of witchcraft, and it has no room in the realm of influence, at least not in a positive way. A charmer's purpose is to attract and allure you to win over your confidence, before you can even get to know anything about their character or background. If you lack discernment you will fall prey to a charmer. Applying a metaphor from basketball, charm is like using a "head fake" in a conversation, it throws you off momentarily, as they make their move to win over your heart and mind. Don't fall prey to a charmer's methods. Charm is deceptive. In other words, don't let a first impression deceive you.

 [26]Merriam-Websters Dictionary: Charm

FLATTERY

A person who flatters, however, draws attention to themselves. You see, a lying tongue hates its victims, and flattering words cause ruin.[27] The design behind flattery is to captivate you through the shrewd application of fine sounding compliments and words. According to Psychology Today:[28]

> "Flattery is dishonest when used to gain or control. It is effective, because everyone has insecurities and loves to be told great things about themselves. Flattery is particularly common during dating and in new relationships, but usually wears off as relationships settle into commitment and reality."

I have personally experienced flattery. At first, flattery makes you feel good about yourself by massaging your ego. Overtime, however, a certain feeling overtakes you like, "Too much 'goose-bumps' messaging—where is the lasting impact?" Don't get me wrong, most people have good intentions with their initial greeting and compliments. Sometimes a person can be nervous upon their first encounter, so they unknowingly use flattery to break into a group or conversation. However, there are other times when a person is very designing in nature. An idiom vividly conveys this truth, "Flattery will get you nowhere!" The meaning of

---

[27] Proverbs 26:28

[28] How Flatterers Can Manipulate and Control in Relationships, by Jason Whiting, Ph.D. June 1st, 2018, accessed online https://www.psychologytoday.com/us/blog/love-lies-and-conflict/201806/how-flatterers-can-manipulate-and-control-in-relationships

this saying is that you can use whatever verbiage you like, but in the end, your intent will be exposed as a facade.

Now, let's move into authentically building others up through encouragement.

THE POWER OF ENCOURAGEMENT

An encourager puts you and your dilemma at the center of the subject matter. An encourager's motive is your wellbeing, not theirs. When someone encourages you, you are made strong from within and capable of confronting your challenge. Here is story:

I remember a time, I was entering into a car dealership, when at the same time, a young black woman exited the doors on her way out. Her demeanor was very evident at first, she seemed drained and discouragement filled her countenance. I then asked her a question, "How is your day going?" She stopped, like she was collecting her thoughts, then all the sudden, she burst out in tears. I quickly followed up, "Is everything o.k. with you? Can I help you in anyway?" She then started to unload her burden onto me, saying, "I qualify for a vehicle based on my income but, I don't have the money for the down payment." She went on to say, "No matter where I go, it's the same thing." How do you console someone who has been rejected several times, because they lack the down payment for a car? All I knew to do is to console her by encouraging her through my own personal story. I then added, "You need to buy your car from a private party." "Why?" she asked. "It's different," I replied, "You just maybe able to find someone who is willing to work with you. At least you will have a decent car for the time being." I went on. "I purchased my car through a private party. It's a 2006 Jaguar with only seventy-five thousand miles." We then walked over to my car. She was amazed of its excellent condition. "Wow!," she exclaimed, "It's a beautiful car!" Tears now removed, I added, "It only cost me, five-thousand. It was a bargain. It averaged less than five-thousand miles a year. It's like brand new." I then saw her countenance change before me—her fear had lifted and a smile from cheek-to-cheek was now expressing itself upon her face. After our short conversation, she said, "You are such an encourager. In such a short time you made me feel so different. Thank you!"

Encouragement has many offerings. One of them is restoring belief and confidence in the other person. If delivered correctly, encouragement makes hope arise within the human soul. Encouragement is life giving power source. I know, in the story I previously provided for you, I felt like I was bragging at little bit about my car but, I was also so excited about how I got a good deal. Encouragement is a superpower gift that rises at the right time, and says the right words, where another person feels empowered by your words. It Is like, if a situation was possible for me, it can also be possible for her too. Encouragement is not a spellbound mechanism like charm, nor flattery; the use of boxed compliments to lure others in. Encouragement involves a sincere act of using the right words, at the right time to elevate another. This action involves a deep discernment of what another person needs at the moment, and delivering the right prescription.

The word *encourage* has the word "courage" in it. So what does this tell you about the purpose of encouraging others? When encouragement is properly applied, you are imparting courage to others. The root word for *encourage* means "to make strong" and "to put in or into." Simply put, you make someone "strong" by unloading the right words throughout your interaction.

I remember waiting for an Uber ride, when I started a conversation with the guy standing next to me in the ride-share area. "Hey, nice day! Where are you heading to?" He turned over to me, "I am meeting some of my friends at a bar." "Oh really, that's nice! Enjoy your time with them!" He went on to add, "My girlfriend broke up with me, and I am devastated by it." I perceived he wanted to chat some more to fill in the time gap before his Uber arrived, so I challenged him, "Drinking won't help you in the long run." "What do you mean?" He replied. My training taught me the more a person talks about their pain and disappointment, the quicker their healing will come. So, he went on for a few minutes explaining his situation, and how he felt about the whole thing. I discerned he was blindsided by the surprise breakup, etc. I then said, "You see what you are doing now?" He looked over at me with curiosity. I added, "You are talking about it. That's the healthy thing to do right now... I call it 'emotional vomit.' You just have to get it out, no matter how ugly it may feel at the moment. Eventually, in time, you will feel better about it." I paid attention to his face as I waited for a response to my analogy about the "emotional vomit." He said, "You are right, the more I talk about it, the better I will feel...hey, someone else told me the same thing!" I affirmed his reply with a "Yup!" His car soon arrived before mine, but before he got into the vehicle, he gave me a fist bump, a guys way of affirming a cordial yet edifying transaction. He got into his ride-share on a much lighter note, of course, and rode off to meet his friends at a bar.

When you are closing a conversation, make sure you deposit hope on the way out.

CHECKLIST:
HOW TO ENCOURAGE OTHERS

☑ **Empathetic listening:** Remember tip #2. Put yourself in their shoes first, before you offer up words of hope. You first need to perceive and interpret the facts before you can understand their dilemma fully.

☑ **Wait for a Kairos Moment:** Remember tip #7, employing substance. You want to wait for the moment in time, when the right time appears before you to speak resonating wisdom into their life.

☑ **Share an Inspirational Story:** Don't be prescriptive right away by giving advice. It may come across as a "know it all." First, build a "bridge of empathy" by telling them your story, so they can buy into you.

☑ **Be Pithy:** A pithy reply comes from the deep well of wisdom. A encouraging word is short, powerful and to the point. A pithy reply from you is memorable because it imparts wisdom. Upon departure please don't bloviate and lose your audience on the way out.

☑ **Unload Encouragement:** At the end of day, it's all about the person before you, not your personal agenda. An encouraging word projects a person a long way into their future by igniting vigor and renewing hope. How will you know you have succeeded? The demeanor of your audience will gradually change right before your very eyes.

ABOUT THE AUTHORS

As a business owner and a former pastor for the past 30 years **Joel C. Garcia** has developed top leaders who have arisen to lead roles in the ministry, and as top managers in the marketplace. Joel is the author of five other books on faith-based leadership, including his latest release *The Gibborim Mindset* (2022 LuluPress). Joel earned a Master's degree in Organizational Leadership with an emphasis in coaching and mentoring from Regent University in Virginia Beach, Virginia.

Miguel (Mike) Garcia has a thirty year background in the marketplace as Physical Therapist and Rehabilitative expert. Mike was nurtured in the prophetic ministry, and is known as a gifted teacher, mentoring over thirty businessmen and women in a weekly Bible study. A co-author of *The Gibborim Mindset*, Mike is currently completing his Bachelor's degree in Leadership from Faith International University in Tacoma, Washington.

ABOUT MARKETPLACE MASTERY

Joel and Mike founded Marketplace Mastery, llc. as an apostolic and prophetic training center focused on transforming Christians in the marketplace with a kingdom mandate and dominion mindset. Our objective is simply to disciple Christian business leaders, entrepreneurs, executives and employees in the workforce to influence and have a greater impact within their respective spheres in the marketplace for God's glory. We offer services in business development, coaching and team training with a faith-based approach to leadership transformation.

You can follow and contact us online through social media platforms on Facebook @marketplacemastery and Instagram at @marketplace_mastery.

www.ingramcontent.com/pod-product-compliance
Lightning Source LLC
Chambersburg PA
CBHW051355280526
45784CB00007B/2963